Green S

GW00671490

59p
2/4

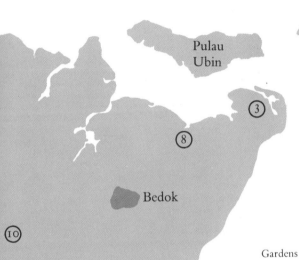

Pulau Tekong

Tekong

Pulau Ubin

③

⑧

Bedok

⑩

④

Reservoirs ▮▮▮

Seletar
Upper and Lower Peirce
Bedok
MacRitchie
Pandan
Kranji
Poyan
Tengeh
Murai
Tekong

Reserves

Ⓐ Labrador
Ⓑ Bukit Timah

Gardens and Parks

① Bishan Park
② Botanic Gardens
③ Changi Beach Park
④ East Coast Park
⑤ Fort Canning Park
⑥ Jurong Bird Park
⑦ Mt Faber Park
⑧ Pasir Ris Town Park
⑨ Sembawang Park
⑩ Toa Payoh Town Garden
⑪ West Coast Park
⑫ Chinese and Japanese Gardens
⑬ Mandai Orchid Gardens
⑭ Zoological Gardens

Dear Sarah-Jane,

Hope that you will enjoy reading this book, specially picked for your interests.

God Bless.

Yours Truly,

Darren

Sept. 23rd '94.

Titles in the series

Gardens and Parks
of Singapore

VÉRONIQUE SANSON

SINGAPORE
OXFORD UNIVERSITY PRESS
OXFORD NEW YORK
1992

Oxford University Press

Oxford New York Toronto
Delhi Bombay Calcutta Madras Karachi
Kuala Lumpur Singapore Hong Kong Tokyo
Nairobi Dar es Salaam Cape Town
Melbourne Auckland
and associated companies in
Berlin Ibadan

Oxford is a trade mark of Oxford University Press

© Oxford University Press Pte. Ltd. 1992

Published in the United States by
Oxford University Press, Inc., New York

All rights reserved. No part of this publication may be reproduced,
stored in a retrieval system, or transmitted, in any form or by any means,
electronic, mechanical, photocopying, recording or otherwise,
without the prior permission of Oxford University Press

ISBN 0 19 588588 0

British Cataloguing-in-Publication Data

A catalogue record for this book is available from
the British Library.

Library of Congress Cataloging-in-Publication Data

Sanson, Véronique.
Gardens and parks of Singapore/Véronique Sanson.
p.   cm. — (Images of Asia)
Includes bibliographical references.
ISBN 0-19-588588-0:
1. Parks—Singapore. 2. Gardens—Singapore. 3.Open spaces—
Singapore. 4. Urban beautification—Singapore.
I. Title. II. Series.
SB484.S49S36   1992
712'.5' 095957—dc20
92-4872
CIP

Printed in Singapore by Kyodo Printing Co. (S) Pte. Ltd.
Published by Oxford University Press Pte. Ltd.,
Unit 221, Ubi Avenue 4, Singapore 1440

To my mother
who imparted to me,
as an everlasting gift,
her childlike pleasure in nature

Acknowledgements

I have several people and organizations to thank for helping me gather the information I needed to write this book.

I want to thank the Public Relations Departments at the Zoological Gardens, Sentosa Development Corporation, the Jurong BirdPark, Mandai Orchid Gardens, Jurong Environmental Engineering Pte Ltd, and the Public Utilities Board.

Special thanks to Professor Wee at the National University of Singapore, to Bonnie Tinsley at the Botanic Gardens, and to Santie Gunasekara at the Zoological Gardens.

I would also like to thank my friends in Singapore, in particular Margareta Cherry, without whose friendship and hospitality this book would have been much harder to research.

And last but not least, I want to thank my daughter Sunshine for taking time out of her busy life as a college student in the United States to proofread my manuscript.

Cumming, Georgia   VÉRONIQUE SANSON
January 1992

Note

Unless otherwise stated and also excepting Colour Plate 3 and Plate 9, all photographs including the cover illustration are by the author.

Contents

1. Swamp in Changi. Lithograph by Eduard von Ransonnet, 1869. Courtesy National Museum, Singapore.

Introduction

At first sight, Singapore seems like any other modern city: a maze of streets and highways, and an impressive skyline of high-rise buildings that seemingly defy gravity. Her population of 2.6 million work and play in commercial, financial, and residential districts, with little contact and interaction with nature. For the first 150 years of her documented history, large-scale destruction of the 570-square-kilometre island's flora and fauna was due to the ever increasing population struggling through the thick jungle, the swamps (Plate 1), and marshes for living space.

But since the mid-1980s, a better understanding of the need for a balanced ecology and a heightened awareness of individual responsibility in global conservation have pushed public opinion and the government to adopt a much improved management of the natural land resources.

Small portions of protected primary forests with 40-metre-tall hardwood trees still remain, as well as about 15 square kilometres of mangrove forest, mainly along the northern coastline in Kranji. Only the Bukit Timah Nature Reserve, left unexploited since 1819, yields the original vegetation of a tropical lowland evergreen rain forest with 160-year-old timber trees and rare species of fern. But with a surface area of barely 75 hectares, the forest is not deep or moist enough and many plants have become extinct.

The largest single area of forest in Singapore is the Central Catchment area (MacRitchie, Seletar, and Lower and Upper Peirce Reservoirs) with 2 000 hectares of secondary forests. Protected since 1910, the vegetation is not original growth, but spontaneous regrowth after the primary forest had been logged and cleared.

The Botanic Gardens, with its 4 hectares of original forest, represents the first attempt in Singapore to preserve and research Equatorial vegetation. Founded in 1859 as the first national park in Singapore, its present 54 hectares along Cluny Road is in keeping with the tradition of the world's most beautiful gardens. The National Parks Board diligently manages the Botanic Gardens, the Bukit Timah Nature Reserve, and Fort Canning Park, the richest historical area in Singapore.

In 1819, when Sir Stamford Raffles and William Farquhar sailed into the Strait of Singapore, they found an island covered with vegetation so dense that only the muddy coastline and the estuary were accessible. Mangrove forests lined the banks of the tidal creeks. The sparse population of Malay and Chinese fishermen and tradesmen lived in *atap*-covered huts along the river banks or on floating villages. Crocodiles infested the waters, and tigers, leopards, and wild boars made excursions into the hills in the interior difficult. A small area bounded by swamps and marshes had been cleared by Chinese planters to form twenty gambier plantations. The Malay Raja, the Temenggung, lived in the largest house on the island, between the sea and the river.

The British settlers rearranged the layout of the land, levelling off some of the hills and using the earth and rocks to fill out swampy areas and muddy depressions. Parcels of reclaimed land were then sold in auctions. Bukit Larangan, the Forbidden Hill, later renamed Fort Canning, was cleared of dense jungle growth and Sir Raffles established his residence there for a commanding view of the land and sea, and to escape from the oppressive heat and humidity of the coast (Colour Plate 1). Fort Canning was also the site for his first experimental spice plantation on the island. This involved clove and nutmeg trees.

One of Sir Raffles's main concerns in settling Singapore was to stimulate agriculture, thus plants and seeds were widely distributed to be experimented with. Consequently, increased areas of cultivation and logging forced a continuous clearing of the forests and the extinction of many native trees and plants, including fifty species of mangrove orchids. The wildlife disappeared with its habitat: the last tiger was shot in 1932.

2. Country bungalows on hilltops. Lithograph by Charles Walter Kinloch, 1852. Courtesy National Museum, Singapore.

An 1848 painstakingly precise government survey lists the cultivated areas on the island: 1,190 acres of 71,400 nutmeg trees; 28 acres of clove trees; 2,658 acres of coconut trees; 445 acres of 128,281 betel-nut trees; 1,037 acres of fruit trees; 24,220 acres of gambier cultivation; 2,614 acres of pepper trees; 379 acres of vegetable gardens; 1,962 acres of sugar-cane, pineapple, and rice; and 402 acres of pasture land. The cultivation of cocoa, cinnamon, coffee, and cotton proved not as successful however.

The increasing wealth of some of the settlers meant more leisure time, and it became fashionable to build country bunga-lows on hilltops (Plate 2) and along the beaches in Katong, Geylang, Changi, and Pasir Panjang. The wide gardens sur-rounding some of these houses were later opened to the public and became the first pleasure gardens to stroll in, or in the case of the Alkaff family's Japanese-style gardens, to take boat rides or fish in the lake, or to race on the first motor-cycle track in Singapore.

2
From Agricultural to Urban Environment

WHEN Singapore became an independent republic in 1965, after a history of invasions, colonization, and other outside interferences, she had already undergone a series of major readjustments and changes. After her founding as a British trading post in 1819, she had rapidly evolved from a basically rural, agricultural setting into an increasingly modern, urban environment.

Agriculture is now limited to 264 hectares (2.64 square kilometres) of high-tech farming and agrotechnological research, out of a total land area of 626 square kilometres.

The first phase of Singapore's development could be described in broad terms as the transformation of a fishing village, surrounded by wild, uninhabited hills, to a small but busy trading town, encroaching more and more on the jungle. Later, plantations, small farms, and coastal villages forced the systematic destruction (Colour Plate 2) of the tropical forest and the swamp areas. Most animals and plants which once thrived there were also eliminated.

However, now that the government has achieved most of its economic and social goals, it can turn its efforts towards preserving and improving what is left of the island's wildlife areas. When the continuous waves of urbanization and industrialization seemed ready to engulf every last bit of natural vegetation, new realizations surfaced: the need to respect a global ecological balance and the importance of protecting the amazing variety and beauty of the original tropical habitat.

The first recorded descriptions of Singapore began with the British settlement of the island. They range from the solemn scientific data of government surveys to the lyrical accounts of delighted visitors.

Because of its close proximity to the Equator and high humidity, Singapore's vegetation is naturally lush, fast

3. Chinese town along the Singapore River. Engraving by an unknown artist, 1866. Courtesy National Museum, Singapore.

growing, and particularly rich in colour and variety. Some of the hills that made up the island's original landscape were levelled by the British settlers to provide earth and rocks to fill out swampy areas. In the nineteenth century, however, Singapore was still for the most part a green panorama of thickly forested hillocks.

The settlement was limited to the area between the Singapore and the Kallang Rivers. The European town had been erected in the centre, and the Chinese town (Plate 3) stretched along the right bank of the Singapore River. The Malay quarter, Kampong Glam, spread along the southern coastline, around the residence of the Temenggung, the last Malay ruler of Singapore. Along Beach Road, wealthy traders built bungalows with gardens rich in flowerbeds, as well as nutmeg and fruit trees. Coconut plantations (Plate 4) lined the eastern coast of the harbour where rice, tapioca, sago, mace, sugar, pepper, nutmeg, coffee, tin, rattan, buffalo hides, and horns were some of the products being shipped out. As a free port, Singapore was a distributing point where 3 million tons of goods were loaded and unloaded each year.

In her 1879 book, *The Golden Chersonese*, Isabella Bird, the intrepid Victorian lady traveller described her impressions of Singapore as 'mainly of overpowering greenery, a kaleidoscopic arrangement of colours, Chinese predominance and abounding hospitality'. She went on to write: 'Rain is officially said to fall on two hundred days of the year, but popularly every day! The rainfall is only eighty-seven inches, however, and the glorious vegetation owes its redundancy to the dampness of the climate.'

Like most travellers of her time, Isabella Bird was more interested in the town than the remainder of the island which was hard to explore. She wrote, 'The island is far less interesting than the city.' She adds: 'The ants are a pest of the second magnitude, mosquitos [*sic*] being of the first, the palm-trees and the piles of decaying leaves and bark being excellent nurseries for larvae.' Nevertheless, she also recognized that 'the vegetation is luxuriant, and in the dim, green twilight which is created by enormous forest trees, there are endless varieties of

4. A coconut plantation. Lithograph by an unknown artist, 1870. Courtesy National Museum, Singapore.

ferns, calladiums, and parasitic plants; but except where a road has been cut and is kept open by continual labour, the climbing rattan palms make it impossible to explore'.

F. W. Burbidge, a naturalist visiting Singapore in 1880, reported in his journal: 'Many of the rare plants, formerly found here, have died out since the destruction of the old forest for cultivation. Wild pigs are plentiful; but the tigers do not often repeat the predatory visits of twenty or thirty years ago, when two or three hundred Chinamen were devoured every year.' He also noted that a variety of fruit trees, like mangoes, mangosteens, and coconuts (see Plate 4), were grown in small-scale plantations, and that 'vegetable crops, here, as in San

Francisco, are a monopoly of the thrifty Chinese gardeners'.

Travelling through the island, he came across some rare and interesting plants like the pitcher plant (Colour Plate 3), and 'one of the most singular of nature plants known as *Amorphophallus campanulatus*, a relative of the "Lords and Ladies" of our English woods; but this tropical species is of Titanic dimensions, producing a lurid spathe, nearly two feet in circumference, and exhaling the most fetid and repulsive of odours'.

The Esplanade

Today, Singapore is proud of her green spaces: they offer city residents a place to be outdoors in the cool shade of trees—a reprieve from concrete. The first of these green spaces was a 4.5-hectare field, a portion of which had been reclaimed from the sea, planted with grass, and lined with flowering Angsana trees. At first, simply called 'the Plain', it was later known as the Esplanade. The Chinese named it 'Twa Kok Cheng Chau Po', meaning, in the informative way of Chinese names for locations, 'the grass field in front of the great court'. It is now called the Padang, short for the Malay name 'Padang Besar', meaning the large plain.

Situated beyond the government offices, the Council Chamber, the Town Hall, the Victoria Memorial Hall, and the Supreme Court Building, it was a popular place for the settlement's residents to enjoy the coolness of late afternoons. The graceful pavilion built for the Cricket Club was on one side of the field, with the Recreation Club bungalow on the opposite side.

A famous 1851 oil painting (Colour Plate 4) by John Turnbull Thomson shows a view of the Esplanade from a small hill beside where the Stamford Canal ran into the sea. Scandal Point was so named because it was a favourite spot to meet friends and acquaintances, and to exchange news and gossip.

In 1852, Charles Walter Kinloch, one of the first tourists to visit Singapore, wrote: 'Between the Esplanade and the beach is an enclosed space within which all the beauty and fashion of the place promenade daily, and enjoy the cool sea breeze. The scene is enlivened twice during the week by the regimental band, on which occasions the old women gather together to talk scandal, and their daughters to indulge in a little innocent flirtation.'

On the far right of Thomson's painting, the white steeple of St Andrew's Church dominates the row of official buildings designed by George Coleman, Singapore's first architect. In the background stands Government Hill, its rounded slopes cleared of the original jungle growth.

The Padang is still part of modern Singapore's layout. While cars have replaced the horse-drawn carriages, cricket matches still attract crowds of onlookers. Scandal Point is gone, and gigantic hotel towers overshadow the white steeple of St Andrew's.

In nineteenth-century Singapore, another part of town at-tracted local families who had enough leisure time to spend Sunday afternoons outdoors, picking flowers and watching songbirds. It was called the Gap and is now part of the grounds of the National University of Singapore's Kent Ridge Campus.

Early Gardens

While the majority of immigrants lived in cramped quarters with no time to spare for relaxation, it became fashionable for wealthier families to own a country house built on the outskirts of town. Katong, Changi, Geylang, and Pasir Panjang were the choice areas to spend weekends by the sea.

But it was in the Serangoon area that a country house and its gardens left a deep impression on visitors to Singapore. In 1873, le Comte de Beauvoir wrote in his book, *Voyage Autour du monde*: 'The one curiosity of Singapore is the garden of a Chinese millionaire, who, having arrived penniless in his youth, by virtue of his intelligence has become the provisioner to English and French steamship companies, to warships, and to all the large concerns. His name is Whampoa. His apartments are built on pillars over little artificial ponds full of red fish, and in a number of illuminated pavilions are displayed superb works of art from the Celestial Empire. The garden itself is a kind of frozen zoo, with its crocodiles, dragons, dolphins, dogs and elephants fashioned from rods of iron, its climbing plants, grasses and mosses. . . .'

Hoo Ah Kay, better known as Whampoa (Plate 5), after his birthplace near Canton, was one of early Singapore's leading businessmen. He used the extensive grounds around his country bungalow as a showcase for a variety of unique plants and flowers. With the help of a horticulturist from Canton, he transformed a neglected tract of land into a classical Chinese garden with artificial ponds, aquariums, streams, and rockeries.

Collections of blooming dahlias, chrysanthemums, and lilies were displayed in elegantly designed flowerbeds, while flowering shrubs of hibiscus and magnolia trees lined the paths. But the most famous flower among Whampoa's magnificent selection was a gigantic lotus from Thailand, the *Victoria regia*, whose circular leaves measured over 3.35 metres in diameter.

The Whampoa Garden was visited and enjoyed all year, but it was never as popular as during Chinese New Year. At that time, Singapore's entire Chinese population gathered around 'Nam Sang Fa Un', as it was called in Cantonese, in an animated and noisy country fair atmosphere. Hawkers would set up their stalls with all sorts of good things to eat, and itinerant carnival artistes would perform amazing feats. Unfortunately, with Whampoa's death in 1880, the property was sold and neglected, rapidly losing its appeal to the public.

Shaik bin Abdul Rahman Alkaff, head of one of Singapore's most successful spice-trade dynasties, owned several country houses surrounded by large, well-kept gardens. One of these evolved from a private picnic spot into one of Singapore's first public parks.

Established in the 1920s, where Sennett Estate is now located, the gardens extended from MacPherson Road to Serangoon Road. Built in the Japanese style, and looked after by a Japanese caretaker, the Alkaff Gardens featured small pagodas, high-arched bridges over placid lakes, and a hill named Mount Fuji.

5. Whampoa sitting in one of the gateways of his house, from *The Graphic*, 1880. Courtesy Antiques of the Orient.

12

No entrance fee was necessary, but a small contribution was requested for boat rides and fishing. An imported live camel was the main attraction, and weekend motor cycle racing by professional riders from Hong Kong and Japan attracted crowds to the specially built track. The gardens were so unique that Malay film-makers often used them as locations for action features.

Syed Mohamed bin Omar Alsagoff's family mansion was also noted for its luxurious, palatial proportions. Sprawled across the hilltop of Bukit Tunggal, the thirty-room colonial house was surrounded by 16 hectares of land, one of early Singapore's most famous private gardens. It included a rubber tree plantation and ample grounds for horseback riding. Three islands, called 'Singapore', 'Malacca', and 'Penang', with brick-built guest bungalows dotted the 5-hectare lake.

Fort Canning

The only hill in Singapore with a well-documented history is Fort Canning. Before Sir Raffles established residence there in 1819, when it became Government Hill (Plate 6), it was known by its original Malay name, Bukit Larangan or 'Forbidden Hill', and believed to be haunted by the spirits of long ago kings and queens buried there.

To this day, the Keramat Iskandar Shah—tomb of one of Singapore's ancient kings from a late thirteenth-century Javanese royal family—is a venerated shrine nestled on the north-eastern slope.

After several hillocks, like Pearl's Hill, had been levelled off, Bukit Bendera or 'Flag Hill' as it was also known, dominated the island's topography. In Chinese, Hill Street is called 'Ong Ke Swa Kha', 'the foot of Governor's Hill', and Tank Road is 'Ong Ke Swa Au', 'the back of Governor's Hill'.

According to the *Malay Annals* (a Malay classic said to be comparable with the finest historical literature), the hill has a documented history of more than 700 years. And in the 1920s, when the government decided to build a reservoir on the

6. View of Government Hill and burial ground (far right). Lithograph by Charles Hamilton Smith, 1840. Courtesy National Museum, Singapore.

14

summit, workers digging around a tree found gold ornaments lying just below the original ground level. The armlets, rings, and jewelled clasps were Hindu–Javanese in style, dating back to the fourteenth century, when the Javanese king from Majapahit captured Singapore and several ports on the Malay Peninsula.

Thanks to excavation and research in the 1980s led by John Miksic of the National University of Singapore, stoneware, earthenware, porcelain, Chinese coins, and Indian and Chinese glass beads continue to be found, further enabling the documenting of the hill's historical development.

From a fourteenth-century citadel to a nineteenth-century English fort, the hill has been the focal point around which Singapore has expanded. Between Government Hill and the waterfront, in an area widened by reclamation that pushed the coastline further south, stretched the warehouses, government buildings, and mansions of Singapore's early tradesmen and planters.

The European community buried its dead (see Plate 6) on the south slope of the hill, from 1822 to 1865. A white neo-Gothic gateway still marks the entrance to the burial grounds. The stone wall that separated the tombs of the Anglican community from those of other Christian denominations is still standing. Despite the busy streets nearby, the area with its wandering paths shaded by majestic, ancient trees retains a serene atmosphere conducive to reflection.

In the nineteenth century, the flagstaff on the summit of the hill announced the arrival of merchant ships. In 1860, when the hill became an artillery fort and, like a medieval castle, served as a refuge point in case of rebellion, a lighthouse was added.

The spring on the south-west side which provided fresh water to the early settlers was used as a ritual bathing area when the residence of the Javanese king from Majapahit stood where Sir Raffles would later build his house. The first experimental and botanic gardens in Singapore were established on the eastern side of Canning Hill.

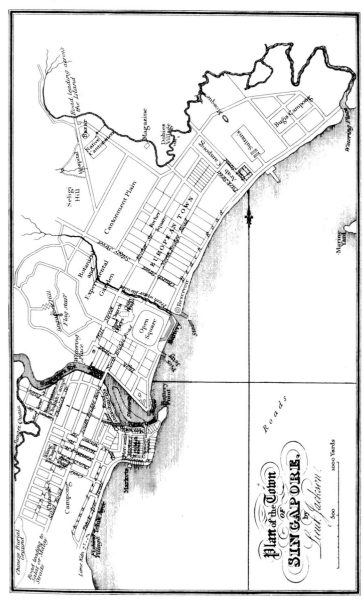

7. Plan of the town of Singapore, by Lieutenant Jackson, 1823.

3

The Botanic Gardens and Mandai Orchid Gardens

The Botanic Gardens

ONE of Sir Raffles's main interests when he settled Singapore was the agricultural potential of the island. To learn more about its abundant vegetation, he sent scouts through the jungle and mangrove swamps to gather samples of the endless variety of local flora. In this way, he started an extensive collection of pressed leaves, flowers, mosses, and fungi.

After the heavy brush growth around Raffles's residence on Government Hill was cleared, an experimental and botanic garden (Plate 7) was laid out in 1819. Three years later it covered a site of 19 hectares, under the care of Dr Wallich from the Calcutta Botanic Gardens, a noted Danish surgeon and naturalist, who was appointed Superintendent.

The first clove and nutmeg trees planted there created the nucleus for the next thirty-five years of spice production. Large durian trees, whose trunks measured as much as 1.83 metres in diameter, lime, pomelo, and langsat trees were found growing wild at the bottom of Canning Hill when the area was being cleared for habitation.

In 1822, Dr Wallich wrote of Singapore: 'It abounds in an endless variety of plants equally interesting to the botanist, the agriculturist and the gardener, with unrivalled facilities and opportunities of disseminating these treasures and exchanging them for others.'

While agricultural experiments proved that coconut, pineapple, black pepper, and gambier were particularly suited to Singapore's climate and soil; coffee, cocoa, and cotton were not. In the meantime, the first botanic gardens were abandoned in 1829 for no apparent reason other than a lack of interest after the departure of both Sir Raffles and Dr Wallich.

8. The Botanic Gardens, 1880s. Photograph by G. R. Lambert & Co.

18

However, in 1859 a group of interested residents founded an Agri-horticultural Society in the Tanglin district, an area then fast becoming fashionable to reside in. Hoo Ah Kay, owner of the famous Whampoa Garden, donated the 23-hectare tract. Out of one section of original land, 4 hectares of tropical rain forest remains today as part of the modern Singapore Botanic Gardens.

Designed to be a recreational garden (Plate 8), the area was laid out with wandering paths, ornamental flowerbeds, an artificial lake, and a small zoo. Flower shows were organized and regimental bands played in the evenings. Carriages were admitted into the gardens, but the horses were not allowed to eat the flowers! Riding over the lawns, fishing, and bathing in the lake were prohibited.

It took about twenty years before a more scientific approach added new dimensions to the pleasure park. The Economic Gardens were created in 1879 with the acquisition of an additional 41 hectares to cultivate a variety of crops including rubber. Started from live seedlings imported from the Amazon Valley in Brazil, the twenty-two seedlings grown in Malaysia and Singapore were at the origin of the flourishing Malayan rubber industry of the 1920s. At that time, half the world's rubber production came from Malaya.

In 1888, Henry Ridley (Plate 9), who was Director of the Botanic Gardens of

9. Henry Ridley, Director of the Botanic Gardens in the late nineteenth century.

Singapore for twenty-three years, became internationally known for his often lonely but visionary struggle to compel local planters into accepting the commercial possibilities of the Para rubber tree. It was only in 1897, when the coffee plantations proved unsuccessful against disease and the competition from Brazilian crops, that rubber became the dominant industry in Malaya. As a result of Henry Ford's mass production of automobiles during the same period, the demand for rubber increased tremendously, and rubber plantations flourished accordingly.

By 1917, the Botanic Gardens had become a major source of seed supply with 7 million rubber seeds distributed to planters.

Henry Ridley was also an expert botanist who delighted in collecting thousands of little known species of tropical plants. He wrote extensively about local rattans, timbers, and drug plants and contributed significantly to the Herbarium collection started by Sir Raffles. A specialist in orchids, he announced in the June 1893 issue of the *Gardener's Chronicle*, the discovery of a mauve orchid hybrid growing in a bamboo thicket, in Miss Agnes Joaquim's private garden. Called the Vanda Miss Joaquim, the natural hybrid became Singapore's national flower (Colour Plate 5).

Over the years, each succeeding director enriched the Botanic Gardens by adding his own expertise and specific interest. Individual experiments and specializations kept improving the Herbarium and the research facilities, as well as the layout of the Gardens.

The 1920s saw the birth of Singapore's thriving orchid export trade thanks to a programme of hybridization set up in the Gardens' laboratories. The method of growing seedlings in jars of sterile culture took several years of trial and tribulation before proving to be practical enough to start the orchid industry.

During the Japanese invasion of Singapore, the Botanic Gardens escaped major looting and destruction thanks to the collaboration of Japanese botanists, in the name of science and conservation. During the years of occupation, research, maintenance, and administration continued with relatively few interferences.

In the 1960s, when Singapore became an independent republic and set out to be recognized as a modern business and tourist centre, part of the Botanic Gardens' focus was directed towards helping in the beautification of the island's environment. The results of years of scientific research and aesthetical knowledge were contributed in the creation of the 'Garden City' image with extensive tree planting and the setting aside of green spaces throughout the city.

The Botanic Gardens has realized its goal to be a world-famous horticultural research centre. But it continues to be a popular destination for outdoor recreation as well. At sunrise, tai chi chuan practitioners glide smoothly through their slow exercise routine. A little later, joggers and their dogs race through the meandering paths, and mothers pushing baby strollers meet by the lake. The Gardens has long been used as a backdrop for countless wedding pictures (Plate 10). On Saturday

10. Wedding party at the Botanic Gardens.

mornings, in particular, cars decorated with pink bows and streamers line Cluny Street, while animated wedding parties stand in tight groups around the newly married couple, against a background of trees and flowering bushes.

The only time the Gardens almost lose their serenity is when busloads of tourists are let loose at the souvenir shop. Before long, however, they rally behind their leader's raised flag-like umbrella and march back to their waiting bus.

Unhurried strolls through the Gardens are best to really appreciate the different areas, so carefully planted and maintained. From the original patch of jungle to the grassy slopes of terraced lawns sweeping down to the two lakes, the 34 hectares of gardens offer wonderful opportunities to admire a wide variety of plants in a relatively small area, and to spot colourful, exotic birds, insects, and butterflies.

The umbrella-shaped American Rain tree (Pukul Lima in Malay), the graceful Casuarina, the powerful Malayan Banyan, with its supporting structure of pillar-like hanging roots, and the spectacular native Tembusu whose red berries feed birds and bats, are just a few of the magnificent trees to look out for. In the moist shadows of the Waterfall Garden, around the cascading stream running to the lake, thrive several species of dark green fern, ginger, and begonia.

Further on, sloping gently towards the smaller lake, the Palm Valley offers a totally different impression. As the most popular evergreen plant in the Tropics, the palm ranges in size from a shrub to a towering tree, and in usage from the strictly ornamental to the factory-like Coconut Palm from which almost anything can be made, from canoes to brooms.

In the valley, rare and unusual Double Coconut and Talipot Palms grow next to Macarthur Palms, the most common of Singapore's roadside trees, with their long, ringed stems and broad leaves. On the hillside, next to the lake, a collection of bamboo (Plate 11) is displayed, from the large clumps of the 20-metre-high Malayan Common Bamboo to smaller bamboos from Thailand and Burma to ornamental Chinese species.

The old green-and-white Bandstand with its octagonal roof

11. Bamboo clump.

is the most prominent landmark. Built in 1860 on top of the highest hill in the Gardens, it still dominates the evergreen landscape, but now glittering metal and glass skyscrapers crowd the horizon. Down the hill, a bamboo fence delineates the small Japanese Garden with its typical features of low shrubs and high grasses, stone lanterns, and lily ponds where carps and guppies glide effortlessly.

Some of the other highlights are the formal Sundial Garden with its flower clock and rectangular pools, the Sun Rockery with its spectacularly shaped succulents and cacti, and the special grove with more than twenty-five varieties of sweet-smelling Frangipani trees. But the elegantly exotic orchid remains the star attraction at the Botanic Gardens.

The Orchid Enclosure houses a remarkable collection of hybrids, some of them named after visiting dignitaries. At the Orchid Demonstration Centre, the successive stages of orchid breeding can be viewed.

The Mandai Orchid Gardens

Several other sites in Singapore are devoted to orchids. At the Mandai Gardens, not far from the zoo, on the relatively rural north-west side of the island, orchids are grown, displayed, and sold (Colour Plate 6).

Started in 1959, on a 2-hectare plot of land, by the late botanist John Laycock, the Gardens were later expanded to an attractively landscaped, 4-hectare, orchid-filled hillside. The best time to enjoy a walk though the Gardens is in the late afternoon when the tropical sun is not as hot. The orchids have been cooled through the day with light sprays of water, and the oblique sunlight catches on the shiny droplets left on the blooms and leaves. A stroll along the curving paths offers a dazzling display of colours: delicate pink, snowy white, golden yellow, elegant purple, deep apricot, blushing red, classic lavender, and even pale green.

In their natural state, orchids cling to trees and their aerial roots find nourishment in the hollows of branches. They are not parasitic plants however, but epiphytes which do not kill the host tree. In the Mandai Gardens, most orchids climb stakes and their roots cling to special scaffolding, in rows of different levels to enjoy full sunshine. Some orchid species with wide leaves are shade-loving, they grow in the cool shadows of protective fig trees.

At the bottom of the orchid-covered hill, a Water Garden offers a naturally cooling retreat for visitors. Reeds, pink ginger, and hibiscus bank the stream which provides water to the Orchid Garden. Lotus plants, Egyptian papyrus, and water lilies flourish in its shallow depth.

Most of the orchids grown in Singapore are not native to the island, but are artificially synthesized plants from foreign species. Since the first natural hybrid discovered in Miss Joaquim's garden in 1893, thousands of hybrids have been created with meticulous care. The orchid-breeding process, from seedling to mature bloom, takes from three to six years to complete.

In the Mandai Gardens' nursery, seeds as fine as dust take between ten days to three weeks to germinate in glass flasks, in a sterilized jelly-like substance rich in sugars and mineral salts. Pineapple or coconut juice and mashed bananas are often added to the mixture to improve the growth rate.

To prevent fungal infections, prevalent in hot and humid climates, the flasks are plugged with cotton wool soaked in sulphate solutions. Later, when the seedlings are three inches high, they are carefully transferred into pots and placed in wood sheds covered with netting. It takes twenty months to six years of tender care before the blooms finally open.

As well as being a tourist attraction, the Mandai Orchid Gardens are also a well-known commercial operation. As a thriving cut-flower export business, the Gardens sell an average of 50,000 orchids a week to the United States, Europe, Australia, and New Zealand. Departing from Singapore's bustling airport on evening flights, the carefully packed sprays reach their destinations the next day, bringing with them the warm and exotic appeal of the Tropics.

4
The Chinese Gardens and Japanese Gardens

The Chinese Gardens

IN traditional China, the four major arts of poetry, calligraphy, landscape painting, and gardening are interdependent. A Chinese garden design combines the essence of nature, movement, and permanence. As Confucius wrote in the Analects: '. . . the wise find pleasure in water; the virtuous find pleasure in hills.' Confucius died in 479 BC, and one of the oldest gardens in the world grew around his tomb, in Shantung province, China. Untouched for several centuries, the large avenues were lined with 700- to 800-year-old cedar trees planted during the Chin and Yuan periods. Unfortunately, since 1907, the garden has been neglected and vandalized.

The philosophy of the Tao is summarized by the realization of unity in creation and a sense of order and harmony symbolized in the art of gardening by the choice and position of rocks, flower arrangements, lawns, and pools of water. Specific shapes of rocks and harmonious proportions of flower blooms and aged trees have inspired paintings and poems through the ages.

In *Yuan Yeh*, a 1635 treatise by Chi Ch'eng, the choice of rocks of gardens was discussed at length. The best rocks are large, with irregular indentations and hollows. The ones with the most interesting textures are found underwater in Tai Hu Lake.

China has a 2,000-year-old tradition of magnificent gardens around the Imperial Palace. At the end of the thirteenth century, Marco Polo described them to be of 'superlative magnificence'. Bamboo and pines are essential features. During the Sung period, 100 species of bamboo were identified. The bamboo represents everlasting resilience and harmonious balance, while pine trees, like rocks, stand in solitude, sturdy and unbending.

Certain flowers, such as the hibiscus and peony, are traditionally present, but chrysanthemums, flowering through autumn and winter, are especially appreciated. Described as early as the fifth century BC, 35 varieties of this flower were recorded by the twelfth century. By the eighteenth century, 300 kinds of chrysanthemums were identified. Along with the orchid, the bamboo, and the flowering plum, they symbolize the four seasons and the four leading qualities of character: grace, resilience, endurance, and nobility. Every Chinese garden has a body of water to balance the earth element, either a lake or a pond where the lotus blooms. Symbol of perfection, the lotus (Colour Plate 7) emerges from muddy waters, in radiant purity.

In Jurong, the Chinese Gardens offer visitors a pleasing and serene experience in tradition. Yu Hwa Yuan, the Gardens' proper name, situated on 13.5 hectares, is designed in the peaceful style of the Sung Dynasty, with some characteristic features of Beijing's Summer Palace. A harmonious integration of architectural shapes with the careful re-creation of an idyllic natural environment is what constitutes the art of Chinese gardening of the period.

Typically, the entrance is guarded by a pair of stone lions. The female is on the right side and the male on the left, with a large 'pearl' in his mouth and the left paw resting on a sphere. In Chinese mythology, they symbolize authority and happiness, and they scare away negative spirits.

The monumental curved three-arch bridge right inside the gates is called Pai Hung Ch'iao or 'White Rainbow Bridge'. Bridges are important features in Chinese gardens, and there are more than 4 million stone bridges throughout China, each with its own elaborate name and unique design.

Another traditional feature in the Chinese Gardens is the moon-gate (Colour Plate 8), a semicircular gateway built to separate garden enclosures.

Further into the meticulously manicured gardens, and past the Hsiao Ch'un T'ing, 'Courtyard of Early Spring', another traditional feature comes into view: the Stone Boat, inspired by the one in Beijing's Summer Palace. Poised and unmoving on the clear waters of a lily pond, it is poetically named Yao Yueh, 'To Invite the Moon'. It shelters the Tea House with its golden-tiled roof.

The five pavilions and the twin towers (Plate 12) follow the traditional balance of height and size so that proportions are in harmony with the surroundings. The structures are linked by footpaths and a winding stream with plants and rocks to create a scene that is pleasing to the eye.

Built on a small hill, the seven-storeyed Pagoda dominates the Gardens. Originally, a pagoda was a simple tower located next to Buddhist temples, but later, it was introduced as a traditional structure in gardens. The pagoda always has an odd number of storeys, and the internal structure may be hollow or

12. Twin towers.

solid. The Ru Yun T'a or 'Cloud Piercing Pagoda' is hexagonal and designed in the style of the Ling Ku Temple Pagoda in Nanking. The spiral staircase leads up to look-out balconies on each floor, with a panoramic view of the landscape below.

Stone footpaths wind around brooks, along small bridges, and through bamboo groves and clusters of willows, to end up in open spaces near the lake. Like man-made structures, green spaces, and expanses of water, rocks play an important part in the balance created in Chinese gardens. Stones are sometimes placed in water to depict islands, or on land to resemble authentic landscapes.

Stones are chosen for their individual characteristics of colour, texture, and shape, and then grouped to create specific impressions, and to bring out feelings of beauty and peaceful strength.

Some of the arrangements found in the Singapore Chinese Gardens are tall, slender rocks with the look of pillars, and flat-surface stones etched with Chinese characters. One such huge rock is called Hsiang Sze Chi Yi, 'Place to Convey Lovers' Wishes'.

The universal art of gardening satisfies a human need for harmonious interaction with nature. In the case of Chinese gardening, the idea is to conceive, in a relatively limited space, a peaceful re-creation of the best aspects of nature into a symphony of contrasting shapes and complementary textures.

The Japanese Gardens

Linked to the Chinese Gardens by a white bridge, the Japanese Gardens, Seiwaen, are located on an island in the centre of Jurong Lake. They offer visitors a chance to get away from the hurried pace of the city and to stroll though a tranquil setting that follows the tradition of Japanese gardening art.

In the eleventh century, the *Tale of Genji* described the beautiful gardens around Kyoto, and some of Japan's earliest poets wrote about the ephemeral beauty of fruit-tree blossoms. The most ancient gardens in Japan were part of temples and palaces. Since the fifth century, the Ise Shrine and its gardens, near Kyoto, have been consecrated to the sun-goddess.

Sakuteiki, an eleventh-century treatise, proposed detailed instructions on garden design. From the meticulously raked pebble enclosures called Yuniwa, 'Purified Space of Ground', to the ten different forms of flowing water, and the complex codification of stones, every element is strictly controlled. Sizes, proportions, and choice and placing of material follow practical and aesthetic considerations.

The Cha-seki or tea garden has its own specific features. Formalized in the sixteenth century by Sen no Rikyu, a poet, gardener, and tea-master, the elaborate tea ceremony required the creation of a small but special garden area leading to the tea house, itself a simple structure with a surface of exactly four-and-a-half tatami mats, a single window, and a small doorway. The tea garden is designed to set the mood for the tea ceremony, and as a stage of transition from the outside world.

The spacing of stepping stones (Plate 13) is calculated to induce careful and thoughtful walking. It symbolizes the path to follow to reach the goal—the 'dewy path' of the Buddhist Sutras. There are no flowers in the Cha-seki in order not to distract from the elegant flower arrangements inside the tea house.

Japanese gardens' traditional features include gateways, bamboo fences, ponds, arched bridges, and stone lanterns for a view of the gardens at night. Cascades are strictly regulated, so their proportions will be in harmony with the rest of the gardens, and with the size of the streams.

The refined art of Japanese gardening is a form of suggestion. For instance, special stones placed in a grove may stand for the omnipresent Buddha and his disciples. The kara sansui, 'dry garden', is the best illustration of the abstract approach to gardening, since there are no plants apart from patches of moss. In Kyoto, the Ryoanji Monastery gardens designed in the fifteenth century represent the purest form of Zen Buddhism's inspired simplicity. As an extension of the contemplative monastic life, the gardens suggest the serene univer-

13. Stone path.

sality of the Buddha's teachings. Also in Kyoto, the Saiho-ji
Monastery gardens, first designed in the eighth century, are
called koke-dera, 'moss garden'. Viewed from the winding
paths, rocks standing in a sea of fifty varieties of mosses create
a minimized aspect of a static universe.

Opened since 1973, the 13-hectare Seiwaen Gardens in
Singapore comprises two ponds, small islands, a rock garden,
and artificial hills, modelled on the gardening techniques of
Japan in the Middle Ages. It is an embodiment of symmetry
and balance, in a serene outdoor atmosphere where space is
harmonized with scenery.

Designed according to the techniques prevailing during the
Muromachi (1392–1568) and Momoyama periods (1568–1615),

14. Pond and rest area.

Seiwaen was created by Professor Kinsaku Nakane of Kyoto.

Right inside the wooden gates is the *keiseien*, the dry land-scape garden whose design is based on the symbolism of Zen philosophy's *koans*, or riddles. In this case, the inherent paradox is that because there is no water in the dry garden, the idea of water comes to mind. And in Zen, the sound of bubbling stream water is compared with the subtle voice of the Buddha's eternal teachings.

The meticulous arrangement of the stones, in their various shapes and sizes, in the *keiseien*, suggests an abstract scenery of mountains and valleys. The white-pebble paths represent winding but unmoving streams.

The central part of the Seiwaen is composed of a succession of ponds (Plate 14) and islands linked to each other by curved, red-painted wooden bridges (Plate 15). Each component of the landscape has an elaborate, descriptive name that thoroughly explains its meaning. For instance, Kyoyochi, the name of the smaller pond, means 'a very pure and quiet mirror-like pond'.

15. Bridge over calm water.

The larger pond, Garyuchi, is 'where the dragon-god, who can summon rain, lives'.

The islands—Eishuto (Ying Chou), Hojoto (Fang Shen), and Horaito (P'eng Lai)—represent Shinsen, the legendary land of ancient Chinese mythology, 'where superhuman beings live and where the spring of the elixir of eternal life is located'.

Each one of the bridges has a poetically illustrative name: Hashinkyo is 'the bridge leading to the Palace of the Dragon King', Jugetsukyi, 'the bridge where one prays for peace while looking at the moon', and Yogetsukyo, 'the bridge which summons the moon'.

The winding stream which connects the two ponds is called Zesshokei, 'the beautiful stream with ceaseless sound'. The name of the stone bridge crossing the stream means 'the bridge where we feel as if we crossed over the back of the dragon'. The arrangement of rocks along the side of the bridge represents a cave 'where superhuman beings live'.

Around the smaller pond, three hills have been built. From the highest, Shiunrei or 'sacred mountain engulfed with purple clouds', a 4.5-metre-high waterfall called Ryumonbaku, 'the waterfall which is the way of a dragon to the sky', flows down in shimmering cascades.

On the south side of Shiunrei, Kakumeidai, 'the auspicious plateau where cranes fly with whooping cries', offers a good panoramic view of the Gardens.

The central architectural element of traditional Japanese gardens is represented by the tile-roofed guest house (Colour Plate 9) called Tenkyokaku, 'building filled with the merciful light of the Buddha'. It is built in the classical Sukiya (tea house) style. In front of the Tenkyokaku stretches a small beach leading to a clear water pond in which spotted Japanese carp glide quietly. The curved beach along the west shore of the larger pond is named Ginrinsu, 'the beach where we see the fish with glittering silver scales spring in the water'.

Ten stone lanterns (Colour Plate 10) decorated with carved motifs of flowers and animals can be found throughout the grounds, blending in with the natural scenery. The four summer houses of different shapes, square, rectangular, or circular, are surrounded by flowering plants and used as resting places with an unobstructed view of the landscape. To complete the natural setting, the eastern part of the Gardens is made up of the Senseirin, 'the forest where many sages flock and live'.

Strolling along the quiet winding paths is a great way to end the visit, before walking back along the southern shore of Jurong Lake, towards Kenshumon, the wooden gate which has 'led to a spring-like paradise'.

5
The Zoological Gardens and Jurong Bird Park

BOTH the Zoological Gardens and Jurong Bird Park* have succeeded in blending harmoniously the effervescent vegetation of the Tropics with displays of birds and animals from around the world. Re-creating the natural habitats of so many species of animal is not an easy task. The local climate is not always suitable for the plants that animals—other than those from Equatorial regions—feed on. Some animals tend to be destructive, thus only the strongest plants ultimately survive.

After the physical completion of each enclosure, the area has to be carefully landscaped with transplanted trees and shrubs. Creepers, ferns, and grass are then planted, not only to create the natural environment needed, but also to conceal moats and fences. Rocks, water, and even dead trees might complete the landscape.

The Zoological Gardens

The Open Zoo is one of Singapore's most popular outdoor destinations for Singaporeans and tourists alike. The name does not mean, as one visitor surmised, that the premises stay open twenty-four hours a day, but rather, and more importantly, it depicts accurately the sense of unobstructed space and freedom one feels when strolling along the beautifully landscaped paths.

There are more than 700 zoos in the world, almost every city has one, but Asia does not have a particularly good reputation when it comes to zoos. This fact makes the Singapore Zoo even more deserving of the recognition it enjoys among wildlife experts and zoologists who applaud the natural and pleasing sight of healthy and well-cared-for groups of animals in open enclosures.

*Officially known as the Jurong BirdPark.

The conception of the Zoo dates from 1969. At the time, the Public Utilities Board (PUB) decided to use some of its land holdings around reservoirs for parks and open recreational facilities. Thanks to the then Executive Chairman of PUB, Dr Ong Swee Law, 88 hectares were set aside for the construction of a zoological garden. So far, only 28 hectares have been developed. But the 60 hectares of leftover wooded land and the calm waters of the Seletar Reservoir contribute to the Zoo, a sense of natural, unrestricted space which is one of its best features.

In 1970, consultants and staff were hired, and in 1971, the construction of the basic fifty enclosures started. Animals were collected from dealers and donated by sponsors. The Director of the Colombo Zoo in Sri Lanka was hired as a special consultant to work out problems inherent in tropical zoos.

In June 1973, the Singapore Zoo opened its gates for the first time with a collection of 270 animals from over 72 species, and a staff of 130. By 1990, 1,600 animals from more than 160 species lived in social groups, housed in sixty-five landscaped exhibits with boundaries conceived to look as natural as possible.

With departments for public relations, education, and marketing, it shows that running the Zoo requires much more than animal-management skills. As Bernard Harrison, the Zoo's Director since 1980, explains: 'The easiest part of looking after a zoo is the Zoology Department; the hardest part is the behind-the-scenes administrative organization.' He remembers, with a touch of nostalgia, when the biggest problem faced by the Zoo was an escaping hippopotamus. The wandering animal walked out of a wooden stockade to test the waters of the Seletar Reservoir. After spending forty-eight enjoyable days in the wilderness, it was coaxed back with food.

The successful breeding of orang-utans is one of many breakthroughs the Zoo has achieved. Twenty orang-utans living together in the type of setting created at the Singapore Zoo is an experience which is unique in the history of zoos. The popular exhibit is situated on an open island which offers both a stimulating setting for the orang-utans, with rope swings and

16. Heliconia Valley at the Zoological Gardens.

1. Dense jungle cleared, view from Government Hill (later renamed Fort Canning) of the Singapore River and Chinatown. Lithograph by Deroy (after E. B. de la Touanne), 1824. Courtesy National Museum, Singapore.

2. Silhouette of jungle treetops against glow from burning trees felled to clear land for cultivation. Lithograph by Eduard von Ransonnet, 1869. Courtesy National Museum, Singapore.

3. Pitcher plant.

4. 'The Esplanade from Scandal Point', by John Turnbull Thomson, 1851. (John Hall-Jones, *The Thomson Paintings: Mid-Nineteenth Century Paintings of the Straits Settlements and Malaya*, Singapore, Oxford University Press, 1983.)

5. Vanda Miss Joaquim hybrid.

6. Orchid displays at the Mandai Orchid Gardens.

7. Lotus blossom.

8. Moon-gate at the Chinese Gardens.

9. Bridge and guest house at the Japanese Gardens.

10. Stone lantern at the Japanese Gardens.

11. Heliconia.

12. Egrets, cranes, and pelicans at the Jurong Bird Park.

13. Mangrove trees with aerial roots.

14. Bird's Nest Fern growing on buttress trunk.

15. Coral tree flower.

16. Traveller's Palm.

ladders, and a good point of view of the animals' antics, games, and behaviour as interacting family groups, for the visitors.

Another achievement worth noting is the educational aspect of the ever popular animal shows. At first modest and amateurish, the sea lion and elephant shows have evolved into sophisticated and professional programmes with an important message. While zoo visitors want to be entertained, they also want to know more about the animals they come to see and they bring their children so they can learn as well. The shows are meant to help people abandon preconceived ideas and to protect the positive image of animals as intelligent, likable, and often funny living beings.

Shows involving snakes prove how well the message reaches its audience. In surveys, snakes used to be voted the most disliked animals in the Zoo. But given the opportunity to be seen close up and to be touched, reptiles have been voted fifth best liked animals at the Zoo in later surveys.

As for animal welfare, recent studies agree that the training of zoo animals stimulates their minds and by relieving boredom, gives them a better overall mental attitude. New training techniques are not based on negative reinforcement and fear, but on a better knowledge of an animal's natural instincts and emotions.

The Zoo continues to improve year after year with new exhibits. The Singapore Zoo is one of only seven zoos in the world with Komodo Dragons. These rare prehistoric giant lizards considered too precious to be sold or traded were donated to the Zoo by the Government of Indonesia. Found only in the southern Indonesian islands, they have lived in the steep, dry hills of the islands for 60 million years.

Along with new animal exhibits, the landscaping of the Zoological Gardens is constantly improved. The Heliconia Valley (Plate 16), an area of about 2 000 square metres located behind the Tapir Exhibit, was the first horticultural development in the Gardens. Designed to display a small variety of plants in attractive and quiet surroundings, it features an ornamental wooden bridge as an entrance point. Small pools of water stocked with red mollies and multicoloured Japanese carps are linked by waterfalls cascading from one pond to the other. A shallow, pebble-bottomed stream winds its way through the valley. A system of pathways allows visitors a close look at the display of flowers, ferns, and palm trees.

The collection of heliconias, a lush, tropical plant native to South America, includes twenty-two varieties of diverse colouring. Out of the ten species of fern on display, some, for example the tree fern *Cyathea latebrosa*, are rarely found in Singapore. In a shady corner of the valley, forty tree ferns of various heights, from just over 1 metre to almost 4 metres, form an attractively cool, miniature forest.

The Jurong Bird Park

In spite of the drastic reduction of forested areas, 320 species of bird still survive in Singapore. Songbirds, because they are small and can easily be taken care of in apartments, have always been popular as pets. Training and displaying songbirds has become a widespread hobby for Singaporeans. Many housing estates and coffee shops have an outdoor bird corner with poles and wires on which to hang cages. The bamboo cages are beautifully carved, and decorated with delicate ivory and porcelain accessories.

The first official bird-singing competition, where birds are judged not only by their singing ability, but also by their stamina and movement, was held in 1953. Since 1982, a National Songbird Competition involving hundreds of caged birds has been held every year, but several local competitions are organized throughout the year by community centres.

Several bird sanctuaries are being integrated throughout the island as part of the overall conservation movement to promote a more natural environment. But so far, the Jurong Bird Park is the best place to watch birds and learn more about them.

On the west side of Singapore Island is a 20-hectare landscaped park, filled with plants and trees, housing almost 5,000 birds of 420 different species from Asia, Europe, Africa, and South America. Situated on the western slope of Jurong Hill, the Bird Park has been opened to the public since 1971. The idea of a permanent bird exhibit was first conceived in 1968 by Dr Goh Keng Swee, the Defence Minister then. The Park continues to add new attractions and to redevelop older exhibits. Its main objective is to offer the public an attractive recreational area as well as a better understanding of birds, their habitat and ways of life. The conservation of birds in general, and endangered species in particular, might be an objective that is less obvious to the general public, but nevertheless, self-evident.

The Park, with its 250 different species, has the largest collection of South-East Asian birds in the world. The new, improved Walk-in Aviary with a population of 3,000 birds, gives visitors the pleasant feeling of entering a tropical rain forest with its sights and sounds undisturbed. It offers a close encounter with the thousands of birds living in the fairytale-like setting. With wooden bridges over fast-running streams, welcoming, shaded walkways, and an impressive man-made waterfall, the 2-hectare Aviary is the Park's most popular feature. A suspended bridge offers a unique point of view over the fleeting, colourful, and melodious world of uncaged birds.

The hatching of the first great hornbill in 1978, and the successful breeding of Humboldt penguins, emus, egrets, and black swans over the years prove that natural surroundings and proper care can ensure that even birds from far-away continents appreciate their carefully planned habitats.

The Park is the new home of birds as diverse as the 2.5-metre-tall, 136-kilogram ostrich and the diminutive kingfisher; the unusual-looking Australian cassowary and the elegant flamingo. A leisurely stroll along the winding roads offers visitors a view of some remarkable birds: pelicans from both the eastern and western hemispheres; storks, the mute survivors of 50 million years on earth; powerful king vultures from South America, with brilliantly coloured naked heads; almost extinct crowned pigeons from the deep tropical jungles of Papua New Guinea; noisy scarlet macaws from the forests of Mexico; hornbills, the largest birds to fly up to treetops, with their unique casques; and birds of paradise, relatives of the homely crow, whose elaborate plumes adorned so many Western women's hats until 1921, that the species was nearly made extinct.

In the 'World of Darkness' special exhibit, modern lighting technology turns day into night for an interesting experience: the observation of nocturnal birds, like the flightless New Zealand kiwi, when they are most active.

At the open Amphitheatre, bird shows such as the Birds of Prey Show, with eagles, hawks, and falcons in free flying performances, attract visitors by the hundreds. The pelican feeding times at the Swan Lake are also very popular with children and grown-ups alike.

The Bird Park's meticulously landscaped open areas and exhibits re-create the natural habitat of birds in the wild with flowering trees and shrubs like bougainvillaeas and heliconias, and shade trees like the Angsana and Rain Trees. Several varieties of indigenous ferns, such as Stag-horn Ferns and Bird's Nest Ferns, grow on Pulai, Chengai, and Bunga Tanjong trees which are typical of the native trees of East Asia's rain forests. Decorative reeds, water lilies, and other aquatic plants grow along the streams and line the Flamingo Pond and the main lake.

Since 1988, heliconias (Colour Plate 11) have been planted profusely around the Bird Park and the collection has grown to include eighty-five species. As a member of the Heliconia Society International, the Park's laboratories now serve as a germ plasma bank. In the jungles and swamps in Central and South America, their native habitat, heliconia leaves have many uses from hut-roofing to food-wrapping. Through biotechnological methods, the Bird Park hopes to develop new heliconia hybrids.

Close relatives of the banana, ginger, and bird-of-paradise plants, heliconias were chosen to be the first botanical project at the Bird Park because of the plant's relationship with several species of birds. While pollinated by hummingbirds in the wild in Singapore, heliconias also attract flower peckers, sunbirds, and other free flying birds. They provide a good supplementary food source for nectar-feeding birds and are also popular as versatile landscaping plants and cut flowers.

For those who are not in the mood or not in condition for a stroll through the Park, the monorail with air-conditioned cars has replaced the old tractor tram. The fifteen-minute circuit offers a relaxing way to view the park.

Built on poles, above the cool water of the largest lake, the restaurant offers refreshments and local snacks and dishes. Shaded galleries permit a closer look at the black and white swans gliding noiselessly just below, and at the white egrets adorning the thick foliage of the trees at the water's edge like giant blossoms (Colour Plate 12).

While the Open Zoo and the Bird Park provide recreational outlets for local families and visitors alike, the educational aspect is well promoted. The prevalent philosophy behind the display of animals and birds in sound and pleasing surroundings, is to educate as well as entertain, without compromising the well-being and the dignity of any creature, great or small.

6

Reservoir Parks, Mangrove Forests, Islands, and Nature Reserves

IT is difficult to imagine what Singapore looked like in 1819, when the entire island was covered with thick vegetation, and mangrove trees lined the shores. However, besides the well-established parks, a number of natural, forested sites remain, scattered throughout the main island and on the smaller offshore islands. They offer visitors a limited but still interesting experience of open areas for outdoor recreation and relaxation. These areas of primary and secondary lowland rain forests, mangroves, and coral reefs are easily accessible in reservoir parks, coastal parks, and offshore islands.

The Reservoir Parks

In his *1907 Handbook to Singapore*, G. M. Reith described the access to the MacRitchie Reservoir (Kolam Ayer, that is, pond of water) as a pleasant drive along well-shaded Thomson Road. 'The Impounding Reservoir', he wrote, 'is a small lake, about a mile-and-a-half long in the heart of the jungle, the water being retained at the lower end by an extensive dam. The reservoir is one of the prettiest spots on the island; at sunset or by moonlight it is perhaps seen at its best. Tiger-tracks are occasionally to be seen in the neighbourhood, this being the nearest place to the town where tigers have been traced or killed in recent years.'

Although tiger tracks have been replaced by 'sneakered-people' tracks, the reservoir parks can still be described today as some of the most beautiful places to enjoy the outdoors in Singapore.

The reservoirs, found throughout the island, are maintained by the Public Utilities Board. These areas of secondary lowland rain forests are popular for family outings by the water, or for walks along the meandering forest paths to observe an interesting variety of plants, birds, and insects. In the forests, trees may reach up to 50 metres, and below the canopy, the tropical vegetation is typically dense with smaller trees, palms, and rattan. On the forest floor, masses of ferns provide protection and cover for lizards, snakes, and insects.

In 1967, MacRitchie, with an area of 12 hectares, was the first reservoir to be developed as a public park. Seletar Reservoir (Plate 17) is the largest with 15 hectares, and Kranji Reservoir is a 9-hectare park with fishing facilities. Lower and Upper Peirce Reservoirs have a large population of long-tailed macaque monkeys.

As for birds, several species of kingfisher can be seen flitting along the forest streams, or close to the reservoir banks. White-belly sea eagles have been observed gliding effortlessly high above the trees, and grey herons, the largest birds in Singapore, are often spotted at Kranji Reservoir.

For even better bird-watching, an area of reclaimed beach along the Changi Airport perimeter stretching north towards Changi Point attracts a wide variety of birds, including migratory birds, from October to March. Covered with low vegetation, the beach offers a good observation point.

Mangrove Forests

Before the settlement of Singapore and the subsequent clearing of land, mangrove forests covered most of the coastal areas. Growing from mid-tide level to the shore, mangrove trees are able to survive in saline water because they obtain the necessary oxygen through their aerial breathing roots (Colour Plate 13). Nowadays, these tropical seashore trees, with their intricate network of interlacing stilted roots, are limited to scattered areas.

Along the northern shore, across from the southern coast of Peninsular Malaysia, Kranji Beach is a muddy stretch of mangrove vegetation best visited at low tide. In Sembawang,

17. Seletar. Lithograph by Eduard von Ransonnet, 1869. Courtesy National Museum, Singapore.

remnants of a mangrove forest have been preserved in narrow strips bordering fish-farming ponds. Raised planks allow for easy walking above the muddy areas. All mangrove beaches attract a variety of birds, but Senoko, at the northern tip of Singapore near the Johore Strait, has a particularly remarkable bird population. More than seventy species have been observed there, including kites, egrets, herons, sandpipers, kingfishers, sunbirds, and woodpeckers. Snakes, crabs, mudskippers, and monitor lizards are typical of mangrove fauna.

The Islands

To escape to an uninhabited tropical island, for a day of picnicking, swimming, and snorkelling, is an easily achievable goal for Singaporeans and tourists alike. Specks of green vegetation sandwiched between the deep blue of sea and sky, Sisters Islands, Pulau Salu, and Pulau Biola are small islands south of the main island, easily reached by chartering a boat from Jardine Steps.

Some stretches of good coral reef remain, with an interesting variety of tropical fish, shells, seaweeds, and sea urchins. However, coral reefs constitute a fragile living environment to be appreciated and carefully protected. St. John's Island is a popular offshore resort destination. The Port of Singapore Authority's ferry leaves at scheduled times from the World Trade Centre's Ferry Terminal. A small expanse of coral reef just beyond one of the swimming lagoons is suitable for snorkelling.

Sentosa, half a kilometre south of Singapore, has been developed over the years as a popular holiday resort island. Hailed in advertisements as 'Singapore's Discovery Island', Sentosa is doing its utmost to maintain the delicate balance between commercialism and conservation of the critical, natural areas of the island.

Formerly called Pulau Blakang Mati, the island was a British military base and a fortress until 1967. It was renamed 'Sentosa', meaning 'peace and tranquillity' in Malay, in 1968 when the

Singapore government decided to develop the area into a holiday resort rather than an industrial site.

Despite the construction of buildings, roads, and monorail tracks, the 375.5-hectare island retains portions of lush, tropical vegetation and wide stretches of white sandy beaches.

Historically, Sentosa's most interesting feature is Fort Siloso, Singapore's only preserved fort, which guarded the western approaches to the Singapore Harbour in the 1880s. The 4-hectare complex consists of gun emplacements, ammunition bunkers, and underground tunnels.

Several outdoor activities available to visitors are swimming, canoeing, and windsurfing in the lagoons along the southern coastline. A cycling track of a little over 1 kilometre long criss-crosses the island. It also runs parallel to the Waterfront Promenade, an area of shaded walkways winding through a fantasy display of Easter Island-like standing stones, grass huts, and make-believe ruins.

The Sentosa Golf Club operates two golf courses on the island. The Tanjong and the Serapong are both 18-hole, par 72 championship courses with a panoramic view of the sea and nearby islands. Some of the holes are set around the shores of a large lagoon.

Access to Sentosa is possible either by cable car or a four-minute ferry ride across Singapore's natural harbour. The cable-car ride, starting on top of Mt Faber offers a spectacular bird's eye view of Singapore's skyscrapers, the busy harbour, and the southern islands. Along the horizon stretches the Indonesian Rhio Archipelago.

Upon arrival, just beyond the New Ferry Terminal building lie the elegant Fountain Gardens. Conceived in the classical style of European formal gardens, with lawns and knot gardens, the area is beautifully landscaped with more than 105 plant species including bamboos, palms, and climbers. The special jets of the central fountain create water effects of different patterns, to a height of 7 metres. It is in the evening, when the fountains are illuminated, that the full effect can be appreciated.

Footpaths shaded by trellises supporting flower displays run along the sides of the 2.5-hectare garden. Corner pavilions and gazebos provide shelter from sun or rain. A high terrace, styled after the famous seventeenth-century Italian Villa Gamberaria, is equipped with a sound system for musical and theatrical performances. A wide, tree-lined staircase climbs gradually up to the Flower Terrace, an open area nestled in a colourful arrangement of tropical flowers. A foaming column of water rises from the centre of a pool in front of the terrace's steps.

A ten-minute stroll through the Fountain Gardens, out the other end from the New Sentosa Ferry Terminal, brings visitors to the Musical Fountain. The computer-controlled system here can play sixteen basic water formations synchronized to music. The waterjets shoot up to a maximum height of 22 metres, and the water pulsates, sways, and spins. The beauty of the performances lie in the artistic combination of coloured lights, music, and the weaving of the different water movements.

The monorail provides an effortless scenic tour of Sentosa. The electric train, travelling 3–6 metres above ground level at a speed of about 13 kilometres per hour, follows the coastline, climbs up and down hills, and passes through stretches of secondary forest.

Several of Sentosa's attractions are geared towards the appreciation and study of nature's many wonders. At the Coralarium, an impressive collection of 2,000 sea shells has been assembled, and the whole ecological balance of a live coral reef can be observed at close range. To watch hard coral feed by shooting out gossamer-fine threads called mucal strands, which ensnare the plankton before reeling it in, is quite an experience. Nocturnal marine life, like the cardinal fish and yellow sea-horses are found in the Coral Cave where fluorescent corals are displayed under ultra-violet light.

On Macaw Hill, in a 7-metre-high aviary that used to be a shark pond, the inhabitants are as bright in colour as they are noisy. Against the background of cascading water, the swift movements of flashing colours and the loud cawing are incessant.

Monkeys, a natural feature in tropical forests, are an intrinsic part of the environment on Sentosa Island. The Monkey Playground is a clearing at the edge of a secondary forest, where rope nettings, ladders, and swings hanging from the trees encourage monkeys to make a spectacle of themselves. Twice-daily feedings attract troops of monkeys to the area, as well as human observers. Free roaming chickens, guinea fowls, and peacocks share the food even though they are not always made to feel welcome by the monkeys.

A 1.5-kilometre walking trail leading to the top of Mt Imbiah cuts through the thick vegetation of the jungle. In various stages of growth, common trees like the Tembusu, Tiup Tiup, and Reriang share the space with climbers, shrubs, and several species of fern. Three species of the insectivorous pitcher plant (*Nepenthes*) grow in abundance throughout the forest. Cicadas and crickets provide the musical background.

Numerous other attractions are crowded onto the island. A choice has to be made, depending on personal interest, between a visit to the Enchanted Grove of Tembusu, the Turtle Pond, the Plant Nursery, the Rare Stone Museum, the Butterfly Park, or the Maritime Museum. Better yet, repeated visits with rest stops at the open-air Food Centre for local Chinese, Indian, Malay, and Peranakan dishes might make it possible to see everything on 'Discovery Island'.

The Nature Reserves

Singapore is rightly proud of its well-landscaped and well-designed parks and gardens, but nature reserves cover only 4.5 per cent of the island. The 75 hectares of Bukit Timah Nature Reserve constitutes the only remnant of primary South-East Asian tropical rain forest in Singapore. As such, it is part of everyone's natural heritage—a rare living museum of enormous value.

In 1883, several forest reserves had been established by Nathaniel Cantley who was then Superintendent of the Botanic Gardens. But by 1935, with the increasing demand for urbanized space, forest reserves were abolished, and the areas exploited by timber companies. Only three of the reserves with a total area of 200 hectares were spared: Bukit Timah, the Central Catchment area, and Labrador Park on the west coast.

For Singaporeans and visitors alike, the Bukit Timah Nature Reserve is a rare sample of easily accessible and safe jungle, with well-marked paths, sheltered rest areas, and from the hilltop, a panoramic view of Singapore and nearby Malaysia. More importantly, it is the last refuge for many plants, trees, flowers, small mammals, reptiles, birds, and insects once found in abundance throughout the island.

The best times of the day to enjoy the tranquility of the forest and to spot well-camouflaged wildlife are early morning and late afternoon. Birds, in particular, are more active at sunrise before it gets too hot. While it is difficult at any time to see tropical birds because of their talent for camouflaging in dense vegetation, listening carefully to their unique calls is the best way to locate them. Different species of bird live at different levels in the forest: at ground level live the babblers; at mid-level, the bulbuls; and at canopy level, the brightly coloured fairy-bluebirds.

Tropical forests are typically rich in insect life, but lizards, snakes, scorpions, and frogs also form an integral part of the forest population. Crashing through the trees and noisily interacting, long-tailed macaque monkeys (Plate 18) are more easily observed than tree shrews, flying foxes, and flying lemurs.

The jungle itself is a patchwork of scattered areas of primary forest, with mature, spectacular trees, such as the Seraya, Nemusu, Meranti, and Keruing trees, and stretches of secondary vegetation in different stages of regrowth, along the roads and at the fringes. Over 600 tree species are found in the reserve. Out of the 100 species of fern still in existence in Singapore, 80 species can be found only at the Bukit Timah Nature Reserve.

Since the deeply shaded jungle provides ideal conditions for ferns, some, like the feathery Spleenwort and the delicate Filmy Fern, grow on boulders; some, like the large Bird's Nest (Colour Plate 14) and Stag-horn Ferns, on tree trunks; while others,

18. Long-tailed macaque monkey.

like the Elephant and the Maidenhair Ferns, thrive on the forest floor.

The Labrador Nature Reserve, a seashore cliff covered with secondary vegetation, was originally a protected area for rare ferns able to survive at sea level. The small patch of rocky shore still provides a suitable habitat for some seashore species. The area on top of the cliff has been converted into a small park with benches and footpaths.

7

HDB Parks, Public Parks, and Wayside Vegetation

In addition to the major attractions of parks and the nature reserves, there are, in Singapore, a large number of playgrounds and smaller open spaces surrounding HDB* housing estates, as well as neighbourhood parks, managed and maintained by individual town councils.

In public parks and by the wayside, the Parks and Recreation Department's army of almost 800 maintenance staff is kept busy with grass cutting, turfing, watering, pruning, transplanting, weeding, and tree felling. Computers keep track of the planting date and size of each tree and collect proper data on health, pruning, and inspection times.

With 4 445 hectares of green areas, and over 5.5 million trees and shrubs, Singapore's image as the 'Garden City' may well change into that of 'Urban Forest' in the near future. In the meantime, the planning and the construction of new parks continue with a trend towards diversity: hill parks with panoramic views such as from Mt Faber Park, coastal parks like the East Coast Park, riverside parks, town parks in public housing estates, and nature parks with bird sanctuaries.

In tune with the universal trend towards a healthier and active lifestyle in a more natural environment, parks in Singapore are conceived with both passive and active recreation in mind.

HDB Parks and Public Parks

The East Coast Park, located along the East Coast Parkway, is a 206-hectare area of reclaimed land, with a swimming lagoon and beaches, a windsurfing club, a rowing-boat station, camping

*Housing Development Board

facilities, jogging and cycling tracks, a golf-driving range, a fishing jetty, and a roller-skating rink.

Regional Parks are conceived as open spaces of 30 hectares or more linking new towns, while Town Parks of about 10 hectares are found in Ang Mo Kio, Toa Payoh, Bedok, Pasir Ris, Woodlands, Clementi, and Bukit Batok.

Nineteen kilometres west of the city, the new town of Bukit Batok comprises 300 blocks of 25,000 flats with small areas of natural vegetation preserved. At the junction of East Avenue 6 and Avenue 2, jogging paths wind through a patch of secondary forest, and a deep pond set in a natural hollow at the base of a granite cliff has been kept untouched. A local version of one of China's scenic lakes, Little Guilin Lake is surrounded by a terraced nature park. A swimming complex, shops, and a stadium, as well as a Thai–Chinese Buddhist temple and a mosque are located on the grounds.

The neighbourhood parks situated between housing blocks are smaller open spaces geared towards social interaction, with sheltered benches, children's playgrounds, and basketball courts. In Woodlands Town Centre Garden, Malay-style shelters and Chinese pavilions are found in the natural landscape of a tropical mangrove area. The goal in neighbourhood open spaces is to encourage the cultivation of lime, papaya, guava, and jackfruit orchards, and to maintain some of the original aspects of rural farm areas.

In Europe and in other parts of the world, public parks are characterized by elaborate landscaping, statues, and fountains. This is not the case in Singapore where the policy is to create informal pleasure grounds with a maximum of greenery and large trees for shade.

When Singapore decided on a crash greening programme in the late 1960s, concrete was already prevalent in the areas of the city where tree planting was most necessary. Poor soil quality and poor drainage, due in part to the regular tidal backlash affecting some low areas, were compounded by the damage done to the root systems of existing mature trees by the laying of underground cables and sewers.

The government decided to plant 'instant trees' instead of saplings, to make an immediate impact on the city landscape. Flowering shrubs like the bougainvillaea, cassia, and lantana were used extensively to provide splashes of red, pink, and yellow in the predominantly green scenery.

In the sections of reclaimed land, the planting of trees, shrubs, and grass is even more problematic. Proper root development is easily inhibited by the high degree of compaction necessary to stabilize the land, and by the poor drainage due to the close proximity of the sea. Fortunately, trees like the Angsana, the Yellow Flame, the Pong Pong, and the Rain Tree are able to survive in unfavourable conditions.

Wayside Vegetation

The greening of Singapore goes beyond the protection of nature reserves and the creation of new parks. From the early years of Singapore's founding, lines of trees have been planted and maintained along streets and roads. Particularly hardy and with a widespreading crown to provide generous shade, the Angsana was the tree of choice from the start. Unfortunately, when a fungal disease that destroyed trees in Malacca in 1885 spread to Singapore in 1914, rows and rows of Angsana died prematurely. Very few of the original trees are still alive today. But as one of the 'instant trees' favoured to keep Singapore green, the Angsana is again planted systematically throughout the island. Reaching a height of 40 metres, with a strong buttressed trunk, the Angsana flowers briefly in a burst of small yellow flowers emanating the faint smell of orange blossoms.

The most ancient wayside trees in Singapore are those planted at the turn of the century to replace the diseased Angsana. Some of the magnificent, umbrella-shaped Rain Trees lining Connaught Drive were planted around 1916. With feathery pink flowers and dark, leathery bean-pod fruit, the Rain Tree was introduced to Asia from South America. Because of its widespreading branches, it is a welcoming host to several species of large epiphyte, from the Stag-horn Fern to the Bird's Nest Fern.

The Tembusu, popular as a garden tree, was often planted in colonial residential compounds as early as 1862. Some of these original ornamental trees with creamy-white clusters of fragrant flowers and round orange berries are still found in the Tanglin district.

Since 1882, the Sea Apple has been extensively planted along Bukit Timah Road, Dalvey Road, Napier Road, and Holland Road. Used as fire-breaks where deforested, abandoned land had turned into waste areas prone to regular grass fires, some of the original Sea Apple trees still survive. Growing to a height of 30 metres, they have large leathery leaves and compact clusters of white, fluffy blossoms.

Before cars replaced the horse-drawn carriages and large numbers of mature trees were destroyed by the widening of roads, a 1924 census recorded 5,626 trees of thirty-eight species growing along sixty-three roads.

Of the other species planted during the 1920s and the 1930s, several seem to have lost their popularity as urban trees. Kapok trees, whose woolly substance found in the oblong fruit is used to stuff mattresses and pillows in Asia and in Africa, were planted along Jalan Besar. Snake trees, with characteristic trumpet-like white and pink flowers and snake-like curling pods, used to line Paterson Road. Acacias, with their small yellow flowers and elongated leaves, were planted in numerous locations before they were officially downgraded to weeds. The African Tulip, introduced early in the century, is another tree which, in spite of beautiful, large, red flowers blossoming all year, is not planted anymore.

The government's campaign, started ten years earlier to create the Garden City image, entered a new phase in 1978. While the systematic planting of large quantities of trees added welcome masses of green and soothing areas of shade throughout the city, bright colours were needed for additional impact.

Since flowering in tropical climates does not occur simultaneously as it does in temperate countries, trees with colourful foliage have been favoured since 1978, along with flowering shrubs and trees with large blossoms.

The Coral tree, a native of South-East Asia, has been planted extensively in the last ten years. With large, shiny leaves striped with yellow, and bright, orange-red flowers in bunches (Colour Plate 15), it is indeed a spectacular tree. The Yellow Flame, a medium-sized tree from Malaysia crowned with bursts of yellow flowers, is also a favourite.

Another attractive tree with yellow flowers is the Golden Shower. A native of the Indian continent, it appropriately takes its name from the way the flowers cascade down in dangling clusters. The Flame of the Forest, one of the most beautiful trees found in the Tropics, is a native of Madagascar. It was first imported into Singapore in 1930. The fruit, characteristically flat and elongated, hang down from the branches. In full bloom, the umbrella-shaped tree is entirely covered with a thick spread of large, scarlet-red flowers. While the Flame of the Forest is a popular garden tree, it is not widely planted by the wayside.

The Purple Millettia, a native forest tree, was first introduced as a wayside tree around 1938. Growing up to 40 metres high, with dense foliage and bunches of reddish-purple flowers, it has become increasingly popular in the last ten years.

Another tree gaining in popularity is the Cabbage tree. Growing wild in Malaysia near swampy coastal areas, its tall trunk is covered with thorns. The fragrant flowers have large, white petals edged in pink, and in an unusual branching arrangement, branches grow in regular progression along the trunk.

Chosen mainly for its straight, elongated shape blending in harmoniously with the vertical lines of high-rise buildings, the African Mahogany grows to a height of more than 30 metres. The Broad-Leaved Mahogany, a native of Honduras, first planted along Bukit Timah Road as early as 1876, is still a popular wayside tree. It has a scaly bark, large fruit resembling brownish papayas, and small fragrant flowers in clusters.

The Hop tree was first planted along St Andrew's Road and

Balestier Road in the early part of the century and is still very popular. The Pong Pong is commonly found lining narrow roads and on street dividers. Originally found growing in local mangrove areas, it has dense foliage, and delicate, white, fragrant flowers. The fruit of the Pong Pong is large and fibrous, with poisonous seeds.

The Jacaranda and the Rose of India are especially beautiful flowering trees, perfectly suited to add colour to the urban landscape. The mauve flowers of the Jacaranda are particularly exquisite because of their ephemeral quality: they last for only a few hours. The leaves of the Rose of India turn reddish with age, and the delicately pink flowers bloom in large numbers.

Since the 1980s, the government's emphasis has been directed towards planting not only more flowering trees, but specifically trees with fragrant flowers. To achieve this goal, some trees in particular should be planted more extensively, according to Professor Y. C. Wee from the Department of Botany at the National University of Singapore. His proposals include: the Kedah Gardenia with its sweet-smelling, orange-gold, star-shaped flowers; the Tanjong Tree with its clusters of small, white flowers used in India to garland women's hair; and the Cempaka, with particularly fragrant white to orange blossoms.

The Frangipani, a native tree in Mexico and Hawaii, was traditionally planted in graveyards when it was first introduced in Malaysia and Singapore. This might explain why, in spite of its beautiful, white flowers with golden hearts and a honey-sweet perfume, Frangipani trees are not as popular as they should be on the wayside.

Common to tropical climates, several species of palm adorn Singapore's gardens and parks, and line streets and roads. Some of them are the towering Royal Palm, the bright red Sealing Wax Palm, the West African Oil Palm, the bushy Macarthur Palm, the distinctive Fishtail Palm, the coast-hugging Coconut Palm, and the Chinese Fan Palm.

The elegantly fan-shaped Traveller's Palm (Colour Plate 16), originally from Madagascar, actually belongs to the banana plant family and does not flower in Singapore. It owes its interesting name to the fact that after a downpour, water channelled along the leaf blades collects at the base of each leaf and may be used to quench the thirst of passing explorers.

Professor Y. C. Wee's vision of the future might seem idyllic, but it is none the less within the realm of possibilities knowing the degree of determination and purposefulness with which the Parks and Recreation Department applies itself to reach its goal in the beautification of Singapore. He says: 'The next decade should see the emergence of a quality Garden City as greenness gives way to more bright colours with the co-ordination of flowering of the plants; and the air heavy with the sweet smell of perfumes coming from numerous specially selected flowers planted for the purpose. The branches of the trees would no longer be bare, but instead, be laden with exotic ferns and orchids; and inhabited with exotic and native birds of many colours, filling the air with their many and varied songs.'

19. Bishan Park.

8

The Future of Green Spaces

As Singapore steadily updates her urban landscape with the building of more futuristic glass and metal skyscrapers and larger shopping complexes, several projects are under way to try to maintain a balance with a greener and more natural environment.

The Parks and Recreation Department continues to plan and create new parks and green open spaces, to maintain the trees and the shrubs already planted, and to do research in soil management and ecological factors.

One of the most impressive projects being undertaken is the linking of all the major parks. Estimated to take twenty to thirty years to complete, the system's first phase joins Upper Thomson Road to Braddell Road with a 5.4-kilometre track. Then, starting from the lower end of Peirce Reservoir, and continuing through Bishan Park (Plate 19), the track will follow the Kallang River to join up with the Kallang River Park. This island-wide network of jogging and cycling pathways will be lined by trees especially attractive to the bird population.

The Marina City Park is another ambitious project, but closer to full realization. This 30-hectare of reclaimed land is part of the Civic District Redevelopment Master Plan which includes the War Memorial Park, the Esplanade Park, Empress Place, and Fulton Square. When completed, it will include a 4-hectare pond with fountains and waterfront terraces, an outdoor theatre, and a viewing plaza overlooking scenic downtown Singapore, Marina Bay, and the Beach Road area.

On the north-eastern coast, the Pasir Ris Park, a regional park being developed, features a 4-hectare children's adventure playground and cycling circuit, picnic grounds, and jogging paths. A wooden pathway winds through the remnants of an original mangrove swamp, and a look-out point offers an unobstructed view of the sea.

Several areas, like the Mandai mangrove swamps, have been listed by the Malayan Nature Society as protected sites, and an 85-hectare ecological park with bird-watching facilities will be developed in the protected jungle area below Kranji Dam. Pulau Ubin, an island located in the Johore Strait, was once the site of thriving rubber estates and busy stone quarries. Now that nature is taking over once again, the mixed forests on the island have become the habitat of flying foxes, monitor lizards, and an interesting variety of tropical birds.

At the Botanic Gardens, facilities are constantly upgraded, and several projects are under way. A garden featuring cash crops of bamboo, rubber, coffee, nutmeg, and cotton as well as medicinal plants is being planned. The Orchid Enclosure will be improved and greatly enlarged, and the nursery will be opened to the public to view the different steps in the production of orchid hybrids. However, the most ambitious project yet may be the building of a 30-metre-tall glass biosphere above a cool and misty landscape of rocky cliffs and dense forests. The 1 400-square-metre area will give visitors the illusion of being 3 000 metres above sea level, amidst the same type of natural scenery found on Mt Kinabalu or at Cameron Highlands in Malaysia.

As for Singapore's historical heritage, the National Parks Board plans to establish the Fort Canning History Project, which will include a museum and a theme park to provide a link between the past and the future. The re-creation of a historic district connecting Fort Canning with the Singapore River would also involve the buildings situated along the Padang and at Empress Place.

The redevelopment and expansion of the sixty-year-old Haw Par Villa into a 9.5-hectare 'High-tech Chinese Mythology Park', and the construction of a 12-hectare 'Tang Dynasty Village' theme park in Jurong are attracting visitors to the outdoors, to be educated as well as entertained.

While the creation of a variety of gardens and parks indeed

enables Singaporeans and visitors to enjoy the natural setting of green spaces, to experience the authentic sights and smells of the countryside is fast becoming a rare occurrence. It is only along the north-west coast, near the Choa Chu Kang and the Nee Soon districts, and along the coast in Sembawang, that the last rural areas can be found. There, from kampong-style wooden houses shaded by tall coconut palms, the pungent smells of traditionally cooked food and overripe fruit awaken nostalgic thoughts of a slower and more natural lifestyle.

Besides the conviction that living close to nature is necessary for human welfare, it is also acknowledged that the responsibility for global conservation starts with local concern for the environment. As more and more forests in South-East Asia are being systematically destroyed for shortsighted economic reasons, it is imperative to remember that the Equatorial region has a special obligation to protect one of the richest and most diversified plant and animal life systems on the planet.

Select Bibliography

'Bengal Civilian' (Charles Walter Kinloch), *Rambles in Java and the Straits in 1852*, London, Simpkin, Marshall and Co., 1853; reprinted Singapore, Oxford University Press, 1987.

Bird, Isabella L., *The Golden Chersonese and the Way Thither*, London, John Murray, 1883; reprinted Kuala Lumpur, Oxford University Press, 1967, and Singapore, Oxford University Press, 1990.

Buckley, Charles Burton, *An Anecdotal History of Old Times in Singapore 1819–1867*, 2 vols., Singapore, Fraser & Neave, 1902; reprinted Kuala Lumpur, University of Malaya Press, 1965, and Singapore, Oxford University Press, 1984.

Burbidge, F. W., *The Gardens of the Sun*, London, John Murray, 1880; reprinted Singapore, Oxford University Press, 1989 and 1991.

Cameron, John, *Our Tropical Possessions in Malayan India*, London, Smith, Elder & Co., 1865; reprinted Kuala Lumpur, Oxford University Press, 1965.

Falconer, John, *A Vision of the Past 1880–1910*, Singapore, Times Editions, 1987.

Guide to the Botanic Gardens Jungle, Singapore, Singapore Science Centre, 1983.

A Guide to the Bukit Timah Nature Reserve, Singapore, Singapore Science Centre and the Nature Reserves Board, 1985.

'HDB Open Spaces', *The Straits Times* (Singapore), 2 May 1990.

Makepeace, W., Brooke, G. E., and Braddell, R. St. J. (eds.), *One Hundred Years of Singapore*, 2 vols., London, John Murray, 1921; reprinted Singapore, Oxford University Press, 1992.

'People's Parks', *The Straits Times* (Singapore), 21 and 22 December 1989.

'Pioneers of Singapore', transcripts of conversations and interviews, Singapore, Archives and Oral History Department,

Quahe, Yvonne, *We Remember: Cameos of Pioneer Life*, Singapore, Landmark Books, 1986.

Reith, G. M., *1907 Handbook to Singapore*, Singapore, Fraser and Neave, 1892; reprinted Singapore, Oxford University Press, 1984.

Singapore Facts and Pictures 1990, Singapore, Ministry of Communications and Information, 1990.

Song Ong Siang, *One Hundred Years' History of the Chinese in Singapore*, London, John Murray, 1923; reprinted Kuala Lumpur, University of Malaya Press, 1967, and Singapore, Oxford University Press, 1984.

Tate, D. J. M. (comp.), *Straits Affairs: The Malay World and Singapore*, Hong Kong, John Nicholson Ltd, 1989.

Thacker, Christopher, *The History of Gardens*, London, Crown Helm, 1979.

Tinsley, Bonnie, *Singapore Garden*, Singapore, Times Books International, 1983.

Wee Yeow Chin, 'The Greening of Singapore: Past, Present, Future', in L. L. Koh and C. S. Hew (eds.), *Proceedings of the Third Symposium on Our Environment*, Singapore, Faculty of Science, National University of Singapore, 1985.

——, 'A guide to the Wayside Trees in Singapore', Singapore, Department of Botany, National University of Singapore and Singapore Science Centre, 1989.

Wong Yew Kuan, 'Creation and Maintenance of Parklands and Recreational Areas in Singapore', (mimeo), Botanic Gardens Library, Singapore, 1975.

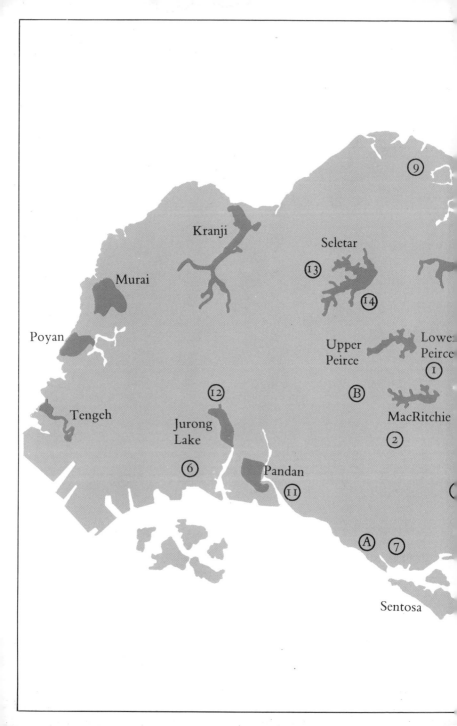